# Favorite Animals
## Coloring Book

## Cathy Beylon

D0311687

## Dover Publications, Inc.
### New York

"If I were an animal, I'd be a _____."
How would you fill in the blank? Not sure?
Here is a whole zooful of animals for you to
choose from as you color them in and learn
their names.

### *Bibliographical Note*

*Favorite Animals Coloring Book* is a new work, first published by Dover Publications, Inc., in 1993.

*International Standard Book Number: 0-486-27727-5*

Manufactured in the United States of America
Dover Publications, Inc., 31 East 2nd Street,
Mineola, N.Y. 11501

Frog

Duck

Chicken (hen)

Cow (calf)

Goat

Pig

Sheep (lamb)

Rabbit

Dog

Cat (kitten)

Fish

Bees

Ladybugs

Butterfly

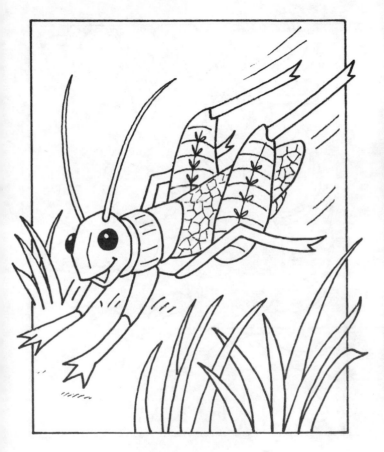

Grasshopper

Squirrel

Deer (fawn)

19

Mouse

Chipmunk

Porcupine

Fox

Raccoon

Skunk

Buffalo

Moose

Seal

Polar Bear

**Bear**

Panda

Owl

Bat

Ostrich

Flamingo

Swan

Vulture

Parrot

Eagle

Octopus

Alligator

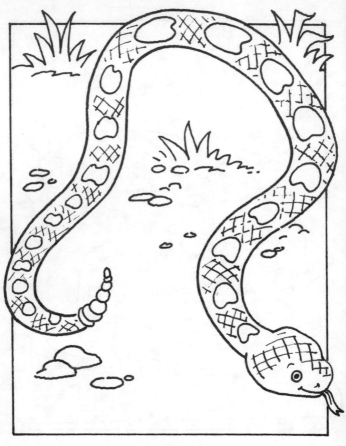

Snake

Lizard

Porpoise

Penguin

45

Turtle

Whale

47

Cheetah

Hyena

49

Zebra

Horse

Giraffe

Camel

Lion

Tiger

Elephant

Gorilla

# Hippopotamus

Rhinoceros

Koala

Llama

## Kangaroo

Anteater

Monkey